FINDINGS

Harriet Proudfoot

Findings

© Harriet Proudfoot 2020

First Edition ISBN: 978-1-913329-11-2

has asserted her authorship and given her permission to Dempsey &
Windle for these poems to be published here.

Published by Dempsey & Windle
15 Rosetrees
Guildford
Surrey
GU1 2HS
UK
01483 571164
dempseyandwindle.com

British Library Cataloguing-in-Publication Data

A catalogue record for this book is available from the British Library

Printed by CMP Ltd, Poole, Dorset, UK

To Suprapto Suryodarmo,

Helen Poynor,

MP, KP, ML,

AH, JH, FP,

MQ,

my family

and all dancing friends.

CONTENTS

Gift

My father lifted me from sleep
out of my painted cot. Held me to him
through a rough grey blanket,
took me out to see the stars,
told me their names, sharing
his sailor's love for them.

Later when he was old and ill
but not yet dying,
I reminded him. He smiled
'So you remember the stars?'

Yoghurt, 1942

Erika Bergmann, small, dark,
unhappy, made the yoghurt.
She was the cook for a time.
We couldn't beg or charm
tidbits from her. She didn't talk to us.

We were always hungry. We sucked
sweetness from the base of flowers,
chewed peony petals, the whites of grasses
'bread and cheese' – young hawthorn shoots,
the sour delights of beech leaves and wood sorrel.

Milk was placed on a shelf –
each step down treacherous, loose
or at an angle. Very old damp.
The toad lived there, wide, fleshy.

Top of the milk rose, a buttery layer
sat in the dark in an attractive bowl.
Wait, wait. Two days till set.
Dusted with sugar, cinnamon. New taste,
new food. Spicy cream in the mouth.

Then I was told to take Erika
half a mile down the stony lane
past the two pine trees, the wych elm
to the bus stop, Hungerford Green.

The Reading to Newbury bus came. A man
I didn't know got out. A man in a big overcoat.
They stood looking at each other, didn't touch.
I could feel the magnets holding them apart.

I had to take them home again.
Behind me, she talked all the way.
I didn't understand a word.
Erika Bergmann left.
No more yoghurt.

It will be all right

It will be all right when . . .

After the cold, the chilblains,
ice inside the window, frozen milk.
Socks and vests in bed.
Running between warm rooms.
It will be all right.

Then we will lie in the wood –
bluebells, dog violets, wood sorrel
and dead beech leaves, beyond the game-keeper's
gibbet. And in the spring the thaw will come,
stiff joints wrench open,
trees shake each paralysed root;
fat buds' scales split, and gape.

Water protected deep
clasp the ice close in your bed.
Hope frayed to breaking,
faith starved to paper bone,
heart sick to feel again.

Love Story

My bear and I would linger
waiting for Edward McGindle.
There were fifteen boys upstairs,
an irresistible lure.

We just got lost, ended up there sometimes,
found ourselves lying in wait on the landing
hoping to bump into Edward McGindle.
I have no memory of the real boy. Fourteen, to my four.

I offered admiration, adoration. Where was mine?
Forbidden again, I sought consolation in sultanas
from the cook, grabbing a small boy's tricycle,
careering off down the road till my mother grabbed me.

So we were reduced to lurking by the sewage-pump
where my father sweated the cess-pit empty.
Sometimes a boy would be sent to help him,
never Edward McGindle.

Then, Fire Escape Practice! A canvas chute –
my heavy father first, then boy after boy
flew down. One landed at my feet
O joy! Edward McGindle.

Bone Vibrations

We children are included, are swept up
in the harvest's wild sea. Men swing and shout,
pitch up the golden wheat. Our one desire
to ride the piled waggons, dipping galleons.
We hang beneath, black with the axle-grease.
Strictly forbidden to ride, we wonder
watch and will the huge horse, leg by leg
straining to start the wide load up the hill.
Hedges snatch handfuls as it squeezes by.

The harvest done, on the last empty cart
we are allowed to bump on the loose grains,
home with this rhythm, this pace, exactly this.

Desire Paths

(Following the recent consultation, the local council has accepted
the public preference not to pave the well-trodden desire path.
– May, 2008)

From all directions children walked to school.
Their feet wore tracks along the tops of banks
above small creatures' holes in the dry earth
past dandelions and tufts of grass.
Their secret paths slipped behind houses
past stink of ferrets, under tall elms,
braved tripping brambles,
face-high stinging nettles
converging on the village triangle
marked by the shop, the pub, the post office
on three sides of the school.

The paths are gone, the banks have shrunk –
no room to walk. No one walks now.
The school is shut,
but in the city, there's the same desire.
Our feet still seek out grass.

The Best Shepherd

Five hurdles hang
from the crowbar on his shoulder.
Five pairs of eyes follow each chunk
of sandwich on his thread-thin knife;
each gulp of bottled tea.
his sheep's black tongues
wear slowly down the saltlicks'
translucent pink stones
in the frosty winter sun.
Grind up orange mangolds,
worry kale stalks. In the summer
lick up clover. He never feeds us.
On the way home we watch out
for the farmer, long to crunch hot turnips,
peel tall peppery kale.

The granary's his den. The staddles foil the rats,
its twilight smells of dog, sheep medicine, oil cake,
the ancient wheatchaff, sacks and working man.

Grey cap, sun-reddened face
astonishing white forehead,
retired best suit, with waistcoat
collarless shirt, black gaiters –
his leather boots are heavy on the pedals
a measured push, dog following behind.
He never hurries.

Summer, shearing time.
He wades in wool and heat
for once neat rolled-up shirt-sleeves,
sheep tight between his knees.
They glide and twist, his clippers,
fleece rolls off in one.
And he can use the hand-shears
with the thousand-year-old shape
and musical scraping click.
No need of the blue ointment.
He never cuts a sheep.

The shepherd has no children:
We children think he's ours,
But later find for twenty miles around
the children all think this.
We know he's fearless – stronger than anyone,
and the best shepherd in the world.

Steamroller

We'd heard of him before we ever saw him
unmistakeable at the little sideways wheel
of the steamroller. He ruled.

It trundled, growled, along the old made roads –
a musical clang over any stone or hump
underscored by the slower hisses of the steam;
the grit swathed sibilantly into the tar.

He stood to drive it, lively bright brass handle
glinting in the sun; he only came in summer.
How could such a tiny handle claim to control
that weight? He was small and smiling,
not just confident, black curls bobbing in the wind –
Gypsy Alf Rose.

The very air of the village was alive
after the dull years since the last thrilling visit.
It seemed to take more years to reach our distant gate.
The smell of tar, obliterating sound, intoxicated us.
We popped black bubbles underneath our sandals
so small grit stuck to them all the way home.

I was a child then. My eye, my fancy can be caught
even now by a debonair curl.

This is how it is

Don't look. I can't look.
Look. See this. See me. Still me.
Touch me. Hold me. Don't touch me,
your hands would stick.

An armour will protect me,
hold me up. I've lost my guts, my digestion,
my backbone, all connection, my core.

No armour, no, it's pushing me apart −
those legs that disappear, not knowing where to go.
Armour, you are no answer. You hurt me.
You're on the damaged skin −
the parts that can't be covered, can't be hidden,
can't be healed.

I will never be together again,
be able to unite head and genitals.
I have no future,
I cannot live in this
I have to live in this

Bed-making

These three red women
are making my bed,
laying me out.
It's a shroud, not a sheet.

They are burying my child's body
the one I used to live in, the one before.
They are soothing it and holding it,
letting it go. They recognise
there was a dying. They accept my death
to my life as it was.

The shroud is big enough for two.
I am stretched out thin to fill it.
They are not taking power
but holding me in love
to let me go
and I can let them.

Then I can come to a new life
from all the green beneath.

Home

We're better now, we fold the sheets
arguing which is whose
We roll the cotton bandages
repeat our old stale news

I make a home inside my head
with sounds of rooks and sheep
it smells of earth just after rain
it is my safe retreat

but what if I get home at last
and home's not there at all
the hospital's long fingers
come prying through the wall.

My leaving present's half my life
I hoard it grain by grain
the other half's nailed to that bed
seeing unending pain.

We're better now, we fold the sheets
we roll the cotton mesh
Queen Margaret's Hospital, cursive script
sewn scarlet in our flesh

Waiting

I

Unfamiliar sound, a car stops.
I climb my bookcase under the window,
hang out to welcome them back.
I see four thin black figures, close together
sad, stiff, heavy. No room for my welcome.

II

Christmas only starts on the very day.
Church was full of green and gold;
even lunch is a little penitential, not festive yet.
Once it's darkening, we can't resist, creep round
outside to peep. Curtains open – the Tree!
Not just dressed, but lit, real candles,
little birds perched, their tails spun glass.
We can wait for presents now, all the time
till after tea.

III

123, 123, 123 – 10. 123. 123. 123….If I keep counting
to a whole hundred, one minute will have gone
from when she's allowed in – Visiting Time !
Here they come – Mummy!

Out

I lived in a white prison –
white beds, white uniforms
colourless covers, bandages,
the ceaseless cheery wireless bleaching us out.

I was taken outside by a nurse, Nurse Mispah:
she had warm skin, dark eyes and beauty spots;
she wore a pleated cap, a scarlet cloak.
We talked. She pushed me

to the shoe shop in my dressing-gown
over pavements, up and down steps.
People shopped and gossiped,
no one lying down. No grown-ups hurting.

My cotton-wool feet, after six months
unconstrained, nude – forgotten –
surprised me. Two sizes bigger
though they hadn't touched the ground,

She took me in a wheel-chair to buy slippers
to learn to walk again;
yellow flowers on dark red velvet
straps round the ankle, a bead button.

Homecoming

His ship is due now.
We've been up the hill to see the masts,
but it's his captain who comes
up the path, and slowly.
His cap is on straight.

He always comes back.
The captain said not this time.
The captain's brought father's presents.
I thought I wanted the shawl.

Invitation to my mother

I want the whole of you,
I want your folksongs looping round
the good smells in the kitchen,
your vigorous clashing of the pots and pans.
I want your flirty, jaunty, off-beat Charleston,
your ruthless slaps to win at Racing Demon,
your 'salty, even vinegary wit'.

There'd have to be your elegant legs –
stockings, not trousers. The tilt of your fur hat.
The way your long skirt flicked out when you turned
in the fawn and cream hounds-tooth check coat.
Your spot-on sense of just what would become you
(not too expensive) and your lovely hands.

Mother, Mother

What have you done with my friends and my loves,
    Mother, Mother?
What have you done with my friends and my loves,
    That were so dear to me oh?
They just weren't good enough for you, my dear
    Stay close to me my darling.

Where's my share of a woman's skills,
    Mother, Mother?
Where's my share of a woman's skills?
    I've looked for it everywhere.
Drowned in my soups and baked in my cakes
    Daughter, daughter.
I skewered and sewed them tight.

What have you done with my lovely body
    Mother, Mother?
What have you done with my lovely body
    My right to love and be loved?
It should be me that goes to the ball
    Daughter, daughter.
It should be me that goes to the ball.
    Don't even think of it, darling.

What have you done with my father dear
    Mother, Mother?
What have you done with my father dear
    That was my other heart?
You dared, you two, betray me so.
    Daughter, daughter
Be proud of him, love him now, if you dare
    My heel goes through his cheek.

Ending

When you died I didn't search
the empty pockets of your breasts.
Your hair was too thin
for my hands to hold its memory.

On Watch

Eight years. Our treads are stripped.
They grind on gravel.
When you died I was dancing
with patients in a closed ward.
I was not with you.
Each day of your dying week
my brother travelled to sit with you.

I visited your slow dying.
Hot, thick air. You tried to breathe.
We tried to find a different rhythm.
Long. Slow. After the jerking years.

At the distant cemetery, each effort
was almost beyond exhaustion.
I need it to be finished, finished.
But when the car cuts in, I cannot
bear the separation. I roar
to overtake, to where I still
need to be.

Missing

Because this wooden spoon is worn right down
and there's a polished slight depression from her thumb –
she always stirred a white sauce vigorously –
Because no one will meet me from the train
or let me find bright flowers by my bed
Because there'll be no ginger cake for tea
or folksongs swooping round the busy kitchen
Because I will not hear her run downstairs
arms out and crying 'Here they are! Here they are!'
Because I don't put parsley on a peeled tomato salad
or cream, angelica and cherries on a trifle
Because her dishes now are mine, but empty
I cannot lift the phone and say, 'Hello, my darling'.

We are introduced

1944. First possible visit of old family friends, from France.
The whole feeling in the dark house warmed. I'd never met them.
I was sent to take one for a walk in the frost. Told she was mine.
My French Godmother. We were polite on our bright cold walk
till we reached the trees. Two larches and a wych elm
where the bitter wind blew from the Downs.
Hoar frost chandeliers. Festoons of glittering light.
Feeling proprietorial, I offered them to her.
She received them, equally entranced.
We knew each other.
Then we scuttled home to tea and dripping toast.

Godmother
(for Claire at 100 years old)

I will make you slippers
of leaves from your lemon tree
with softest linings made of love of poetry.
I will knit a patterned waistcoat
of all our favourite jokes,
the ones each of us knows
the other one will like –
the ones I save up for you.

I will sew you wrist-bands
of many years of sun
knowing each other's lives and families;
of pleasures and adventures we have shared:
Brittany, France, Le Maroc, Tunisie.

I will embroider gloves for you,
small ones to fit your hands
to keep you from the cold
with orange, terra-cotta, scarlet –
the colours you delight in
and sequins of the colours of the sea.

I'll find a cedar cone and make a pendant
smelling of pine and opening like a rose;
design a gown of poppies and ranunculus
with fiery waistband of crocosmia,
first growing in your garden, now in mine.

The statuary of sheets

Winds make sand waves.
Miles inland, a tractor's furrows,
White with seagulls.

Sheets dry on lavender, on sweet briar,
absorb green apple taste.
Double sheets on the line
we true them up, from me to you,
from you to me.

Prospero's robe carries his role.
Cloth's weight embodies his authority,
his power, his presence.

Movement is petrified in Christ in majesty,
cathedrals' saints, Chartres, Notre Dame.
Stillness holds sanctity, power perpetual.

Waves of the Virgin's hair almost smell sweet.
Mary, in flowing stone, offers her breast.

White sheets in a deep bath,
their owner dying. My back
strains with the wet weight.
To wash them, such a puny tenderness
for a dying artist. The folds
create and recreate beauty so brief
even she will survive it.

Leaving
(i.m. R)

You kissed me gently on the cheek, and left.
I hadn't noticed you among the other dancers.

How did you know we'd fit so well together
in all the next year's dancings? You looked for me.

When did I notice your almost black hair,
its layers of fire?

Next year, nine days – dancers moved together and apart.
On the last night, English rhythms, African balafons

carried us all up and away – wound tight, intoxicated,
the energy unstoppable.

Only late, very late, spins slowed, dancers crept out.
You took my hand. Past hedges flashing dew,

rich, damp earth smells, light hinting its return.
My room. Hair in a brush, a bitten apple.

Shamed, I hesitate, turn away. You turn too,
and leave. Regret beats at my head all night.

A year. Another. I was digging, planting,
in my North London garden, Arsenal's roar a distant purr.

Invisible, unmistakable, you flew down above me twice.
On your way.

'It's been so lovely and pleasant to know you.'
(i.m. D.V.)

What is gone? Her welcome.
Familiar smell of home.
The house-tall tree I planted. Her face.

My tree's dancing grace. Her music.
Undaunted travelling. Her courage.
Early pain. Lifelong pain.
Light-switches within reach in the dark.
Familiar sounds from next door.
The iron fireplace, ripples polished to steel.
Her steadfastness. Her listening.
Fitting the space in each room. Ongoing dialogue.
Her patience. Knowing each year where
invisible flowers will appear and when –
having the right to pick them.
Shared jokes, shared tastes. Pursuing healing.
Seven am drive to Communion – 'Come too and swim!'
Shared past, unshared past.
Her discipline. A distant intimacy.
Anxiety – roof, damp, electrics. Abrasiveness.
Upkeep responsibilities. Not suffering fools.
Twelve steep garden steps. Impatience.

Shock of days of body full of tears.

Not gone – wisdom, balance, love, her face, her voice.

Let go.

Not yet.

Morning Star

Sing a lament for Edisher
the eager, upright gentle man.
Trusted in the wild villages,
in the far mountains, welcome.
The passionate perfectionist, beloved.

He sang and taught his country's music
so hard to learn and ravishing to hear.
Collected songs of the year-long work:
digging, planting, harvests –
and feasts and toasts, wild dancing,
daggers thrown into the singing circle,
soft boots stamping men's challenges.

Even these songs cannot heal him now.
Let the men's tender voices
sing a lament for a dead son –
may he rest in peace.

*Edisher Garakanidze, Georgian musicologist, Singer, Teacher,
Conductor of the Men's Choir MTIEBI, the Morning Star. Died
September, 1998.*

A month since she died

In my allotted convent room,
before I met her, I found ceratostigma, caryopteris,
blue-grey October flowers and dark red leaves ;
I hadn't known she was the convent gardener.

Pairs of black habits processed into the chapel,
I saw her graceful genuflexion to the floor
and knowing she was a dancer,
guessed who she was among the other sisters.

We talked in gaps between the Offices,
Lauds, Matins, Vespers. Daily
soaring lines of women's voices
lift prayers through all the seasons.

We sat and talked under a red-leaved prunus,
together trimmed a winter-flowering shrub,
she in her pale-blue garden trousers,
one with the shears, and one to judge the shape.

After my last goodbye, I walk the round again
recognize our bush, viburnum, leafless now.
In the damp cold, little pink tips of buds
are opening as they should.

Purple Lipstick

Painter's Lane, one place we never went.
We'd tiptoed half-way down once, seen no-one.
Found no houses, scared ourselves back up
with its very reputation. The unseen gamekeeper!

So how did I find myself at the top of it?
We were never allowed so far from home, not alone.
Certainly I was lonely. Two little brothers
aren't enough, are not a girl, my age, to play with.

Suddenly, 'Boo!' I was jumped from behind.
A huge smile saying, 'Have some. Look! There's lots,
No one to stop us.' Ripe blackberries everywhere,
their straggling hoops untouched.

Black, glowing. So many, no need to pretend
a half-ripe one was sweet enough, or hope
a blowsy grey one had some goodness left –
and no maggots.

'Let me make you up' she said. I gave her purple eyebrows.
Purple lipstick for me. We sang, 'You are my sunshine!'
and danced. We made each other crowns of Travellers' Joy
and slashed down nettles on our chargers.

We had a shouting competition – no one to tell us off.
Then we were near the road. We found apples, sweet and ripe,
an enclosed space, plants run to seed and broken walls.
A house had been here. This 'No House' would be our home forever.

I don't remember how or when we parted,
faces painted, hankies dripping purple juice.
Did she even have a name? Did I notice what she wore?
For once, we'd had enough, sated with the abandon of the day.

Best Friend 1948

Her house was near my long way home.
No friends where I lived – the last girl off the bus.
Once a year, perhaps, a special treat,
I was invited. Her mother would let us make
delicious biscuits – a most rare treat
just after the war.

There was a huge dressing-up box,
a gold tunic, embroidered waistcoat,
purple gauze turban with a jewelled crest,
soft green silk pantaloons.
We could be anyone. I could be Theseus,
she Hippolyta, in our school play.

We could let rip, sing, shout, dance
up and down the stairs. Her father,
tall and rather stern, as fathers were
in those days – he'd been a judge in India –
was nowhere to be seen.

At last I could invite her to my house.
There were 'white rats', iced buns for tea.
One each. We tried dressing up.
No Indian wonders to wear, but my friend
was in my house.

We played too long. I got too happy,
raced up and down the stairs.
My mother tried to stop us, her father waiting.
I couldn't stop, wanted to keep her
forever. Mother invoked my huge, angry father.
I hid my friend in a cupboard. He flung it open.

She never came again.

The Truce is Ended

Feel the spring of the thyme-turf under our feet. Feel the wind
from over the Downs gather declivities,
the rounded hills, bringing its sweet smell. Feel it, stand
against it, be lifted by it – lie back on it.
Reach up to the larks. Follow each one's note
till you can see the bird – the source, high high
on the edge of the cloud.

White violets from behind the hedgerow,
bryony, Traveller's Joy from the lane. Gold,
purple Pasque flower, harebells, helianthemums
for you.

Come with me now, though we fought for so long
to V.E. Night. *Peace*. To the edge, beyond
the high bonfire. Away from its light.
There, something new. From invisible villages,
noiseless fireworks inching up.

The water is wide

The winter ferry on the Rhine,
still working between snow and storms.

Steps down and a coin for the ferryman.
I leave the rich city's overhang.

He steers by the current, his cord still attached
to the mother-wire linking the banks. No engine –
drifting, held in tension, with purpose to cross.

Through the planks, the water's movement
 reaches, soothes. I am held, safe, can let go,
rocked. The pleasure.

We will land and find the millpool in the sun –
deep, transparent, silent, still.

The millrace in the distance.

Tilleul

Wide wooden stairs to the very top
sun blinding from tall windows.

We swim through dry, sweet fog
crunch over gritty layers – tisane
a floor of lime flowers drying for digestion.

We find and wind a wax cylinder phonograph;
a family voice, brittle and dry,
comes down the decades.

A comic song by a great-grandfather. He ends
'Vive le Papa Richard' and laughs.
Long live his long-dead voice.

Incident

We lived near the Downs.
'No, Ups,' I said when I was four.
Older, we never questioned going up alone.
There was a quarry with friable clay sides –
a surprise in all that chalk and flint
where my brothers used to dig to China.
The sides had velvet helianthemums
short-lived little suns and sunsets.
A hawthorn tree grew out of a low mound
by itself in the middle of the quarry.
Unaware, I lay down under it. I didn't sleep
and no one came. I became one
with the universe.

Invasion

Rumble in the distance. Nearer,
clanking roar as it goes past.
House vibrates to it roots,
papers dance on top-floor desk.

Trundling, old familiar music
steamroller, and its pup.
Surveillance on each move,
ton-weight precise machines.

Men in yellow jackets, white helmets
tiny, high above each one's machine,
look down each side, verify their result.
Long lorry slowly tips amalgam in the spreader.

Rollers move in smoothly,
tar almost instantly solid.
I breathe in the hot road
feet appliquéd to the surface.

Men in boots trim the blackstuff
tight to the pavement with shovels.
The stately convoy leaves,
sounds recede round the corner.

Found Poem

Lady's smocks in the grass, rushes, three-sided sedge,
dry underfoot in the damp places. Insidious brambles lie in wait
Bugle, yellow pimpernel, primrose – bluebells and two white.
The deer have been culled – re-growings now – look!
Twin cup-shaped cavities – deep green cotyledons, pointed shoots between.
Little brown oak leaves, close to the ground, reach outwards.
Transparent copper leaves wave thinly in the sun.
Whitish buds struggle upwards – honeysuckle.
Wood sorrel is sour. Wild garlic hot
self-heal, stitchwort, chickweed, speedwell,
anemone nemorosa, Queen Anne's Lace.
From the window in the night, white grass – white frost.

Caught

One drop of yesterday's rain
under a curving twig
reminds me of diamonds hanging
all across chicken wire – or rain at night,
veiling or blown across
the street light.

Thirst

Road menders break a main –
no water in all the street. Empty taps coughing,
paralysis like cold. Parched skin – dehydration,
losing balance. Fear, though the water will be back tonight.

Forked fountain in my garden – cut water main.
Neighbours stagger in a huge transparent box
half full. Midday sun catches its pool –
light in the waterless dark.

By the evening, hands under running water,
face full of its gift. Dowse face
into floating mosses, cool tickle, breathless.
Streams on the Moor sing, guggle their way to the Dart.

The Char reaches its goal, still pouring
though turned sideways by the sea.
Tide chuckles in under stones, round rocks
crepitation of blue lias ribbons over sand.

I wear a necklace of sea glass
so I can always hear the sea.

Reeling in

Warm hand in the imperceptibly
warm stream. Fish visible, some still.
Blue scales, green, pink, swim at their own level.
Hand and fish exchange caresses.
In Monterey, little jellyfish
flounce, pulsate, glow.

Dark. Heavy mood and evening light. Ilha Bella.
Round a sudden corner, frenzied flashes, speedings –
little boats, lights at their masts, twist, drive forward.
The night tide is up, brings the fish.
Boats jostle, force their way, compete,
dart across between each other, shout –
just below us. Almost ram the jetty.
Now I'm awake, alive in Brazil.

The Char pours down, flow turned by the sea.
Tide comes up, slapping against the sea wall,
brings up the big fish and the fishermen.
Each line is anchored, bucking with the waves.
Each man has his tent of light, himself
still in the dark. Across the estuary,
an echo, smaller tents of light – diminishing.

Nacre

Nacreous oyster shell,
almost transparent, reflecting light.
A less translucent patch inside,
a little rough recess, split from its twin.
Pink almost to purple, cool, smooth
polished, buffed. A curved hand
holding holy water - pilgrim's
life-saving water scoop. A silk skirt
flowing in tiers, inside out.
Scatter of purple sand behind the shine.
Layers of laid-down opalescence,
mother of pearl.

Not For Sale

(After the sculpture by Nicola Hicks)

Exhibition figures. Room full of their life-sized presence.
All straw and clay – wolf, woman in long skirt, red apron.

Separate, round a corner, a surprise,
on a table, an unglazed head, red clay.

A baby, still wet almost, almost with wisps of caul,
infinitely old, come from the start of time.

Sculptor mother got up to catch its look
of astonishment at its journey.

Spring fed

(from 'Spring Fed'*, a painting by Andrew Wyeth*)

From glints on metal, light on water
grey-white, yellow-white
a song in every grey,
to the dark bar, the shadow
and the rich stone trough.

This place is practical.
The length of wire moors the waiting pail.
The bucket's burnished clean,
the cup is ready and the water clear and cool
and always moves – receives and gives
unfailing like the spring in Spain – Mas can Salavia.
Stretches for ever from the distance
where the trees cover the foothills.
'La laine de la montagne' – said our host
who'd been a shepherd in his youth.

(la laine de la montaigne – the mountain's fleece)

Summer Solstice

I want to dance from here to Avebury
the whole stone circle, every megalith.
Lost in the ditch, flying the chalk bank
rooks above, jackdaw below.
Foxtail, leatherleaf, slicing couch.

Tread down a circle in the grass –
spangletop, squirrel tail, timothy
sharp juicy smells under our feet
cool stalks between our toes –
an audience space for witnessing the dance.

Touch the stone's age, two arms' length wide
white giant, rough under fingers, sparkling.
Late, it's still light. Rooks fan their way home.
Move in the space between the two clocks' striking.
Tufted, quaking, cocksfoot, sedge.

Rodin Dancing

The sweetest dressing of the day is the undressing
peeling off, freeing from mummy bands
the animal, the soul.

Silk so fine it billows softly down,
intangible as scarves cut through unhurt by Saladin,

Soft as translucencies round Khmer dancers,
who pose for him, on the long train to Marseille
for the boat home to Cambodia.

Through his hands, he apprehends character,
quality, portraits, feeling. Presents these
through solid clay or hard, dark bronze.

The Gates of Hell, The Burghers of Calais
are dense.

Here, he's after life and movement
his hands find different means,
soft pencil, washes of aquarelle:
he's joined their dance.

Moving Still

(For Helen and Prapto and all dancing friends)

In my garden, eleven pale orange poppies
bounce with the bustle and rummage of the bees
whose weight unbalances each one in turn.
Cool silk chiffon petals, almost impalpable
between my fingers, are gone by midday.
The violence and variety of the wind create
perpetual dance.

The one boy in the dancing class,
back stiff against the wall
was gone next week.
But for me, every minute was delight
And the final polka – the magic,
when Miss Barrett flew
each of us all round the room –
was heaven – beyond ecstasy!

Then I was in hospital
my legs in half splints to keep them straight.
Suddenly an irresistible tune on the dreary wireless.
I hadn't been out of bed for months. I got my legs
over the side. They danced, in their splints. At the end
I pulled them back. No one saw.

Since then, many kinds of dance, many dancings.
Scottish is tricky. English Playford too, Barn Dance is freer.
Best of all is movement in meditation, by the sea –
open. wide, free – in the land, in the wind
moving with the wind in the barley
moving with the moving earth.

Winter dancing

Padded jackets, baggy trousers, scarves, hats
boots. They emerge. Bushelled shafts of light.
Covered wells of life. Glimmers of divinity
carry their treasure disguised.

Touching without touching,
meeting without words
soles bare, black,
sweat drops on the floor.

The beat is the water to swim in.
Circle, pirouette, caracole, leap.
Thread through the bodies.
They meet the sound, create the dance.

Room full of movement,
dance creates, reveals the dancer
in the moving mirror. Essential selves.
Distant, closer than words.

Music softens. Gradually,
vibrations die away.
Dancers find their endings,
stop, rest, dress, leave.

Padded jackets, baggy trousers, scarves, hats,
boots. They emerge. Bushelled shafts of light.
Covered wells of life. Glimmers of divinity
carry their treasure disguised.

Ginkgo biloba
Survivors of Hiroshima

We are old. Palaeolithic.
Two hundred million years.
Tall, one hundred feet.
Unique species. Maidenhair tree.
Our fair hair floats in the little wind.

Six of us near the hypocentre.
Pressure, five tons, temperature
three hundred thousand degrees.

We knew we were resistant to wind
snow, insects, disease, to frost.
We found we can live through fire.

Leaves gone, twigs. Branches like claws,
bark melted into rivulets, parallel currents.
We are hibakusha, eyes fused shut.

Slowly we creak off the shock,
re-find our trunks. Begin
to recognise their changes,
dare to think of growing.
Sap inches through the branches,
dares to resurrect the seed.

See our green skirts of aerial roots
excited by disturbance into life,
the pale gold light through
our two-fold fans –
these hold our story now.

ACKNOWLEDGEMENTS

Acknowledgements are due to the editors of the following publications:

Anthologies: *As Girls Could Boast* (Oscars Press, 1994); *Not Only The Dark* (Categorical Books, 2011); *Through a Child's Eyes: Poems from World War II* (Poetry Space, 2013; *Fanfare* (Second Light, 2015); *Alternative Truths* (Dempsey & Windle, 2019);

Magazines: *Artemis Poetry*; *Smiths Knoll*; *Staple*; *The French Literary Review.*

'Ginkgo biloba' won the Second Light Poetry Short Poem Competition in 2019.

My poem 'The Whole Room Was Skin' was published on the 73 London bus in 2005.

THANKS

Warm thanks to: Michael Laskey and Joanna Cutts for their generous suggestions; Katherine Gallagher for her Torriano Poets and for her experienced support; all members of Tideway poetry group for years of much valued sustaining criticism and the lively and perceptive Forest Poets Stanza Group, and Jane Draycott for her discernment and Michael Symons Roberts for his, both of these on Arvon courses.